ISBN: 978-1-957319-01-8 (Paperback)

Library of Congress Control Number: 2021924749

Any references to historical events, real people, or real places are used fictitiously. Names, characters, and places are products of the author's imagination.

Printed in the United States of America.

First printing edition 2022

Publisher

J.C. Preston
8297 Champions Gate Blvd, #387
Champions Gate, FL 33896

www.skyandria.com

To my wonderful husband Richard, Thank you for all the love and support you have given me throughout the years. To my sisters, Linda and Marie, thank you for the words of encouragement. To my beautiful daughter Ria, thank you for the inspiration.

MY NAME IS

Hi, my name is Ria. This is my twin brother Sky. Do you remember how you learned to crawl, to stand, to walk? It's ok, we did not remember either. That's why we asked our mommy.

Our mommy said before we learned to sit, crawl, or walk, we had to strengthen our neck, back, and leg muscles. I asked, "how did we do it mommy?" She said, "you and your brother did lots and lots of tummy time!"

We did tummy time EVERYDAY! After a few weeks, our neck, our back, and shoulder muscles became strong.

Monday

Tuesday

Wednesday

Thursday

Friday

Saturday

Sunday

Soon, we were strong enough to sit up without falling over when mommy propped us up with pillows. If and when we fell down, our mommy would kiss us, add more pillows, and then sit us up again.

When mommy removed the pillows, we would slouch, then we would fall. When we fell, we would rock from side to side. That is how we learned to roll!

We would roll around all day. Then, we started to pull forward with our arms, while pushing with our legs. That is how we learned to scoot!

Whenever mommy picked us up, we would dangle our legs, bounce up and down, and push against her with our feet. Mommy said Sky and I really enjoyed doing that.

When mommy put us on the floor, we would push up onto our hands, while pushing out with one knee bent, and the other knee extended. That is how we learned to crawl!

We would crawl from the bedroom to the livingroom. We would crawl around the couch and the living room table. We would crawl everywhere and touch everything!

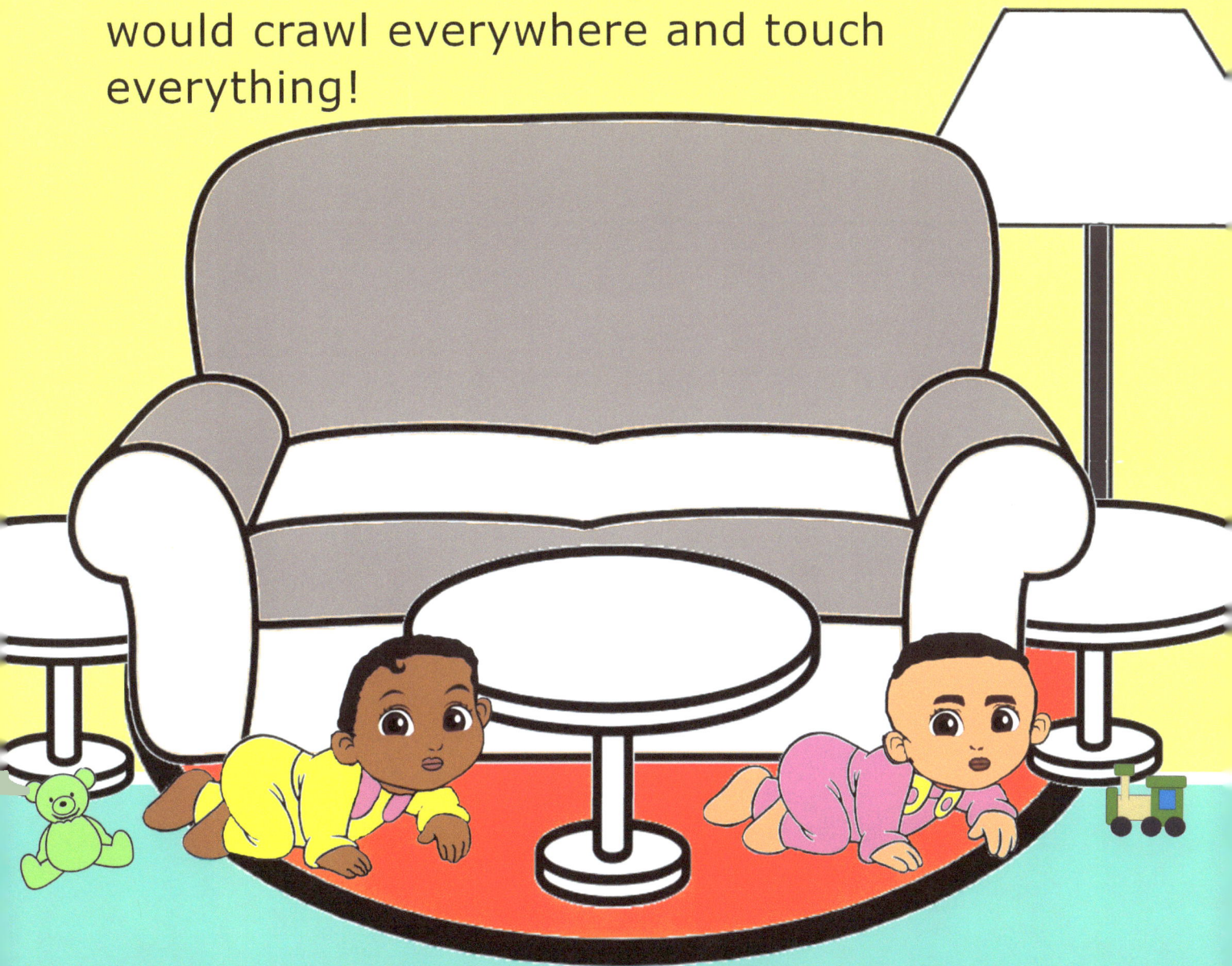

Mommy and Daddy started to childproof our house. They hid the power cords and put covers on all the outlets. At first, we were sad that we could not play with the plugs. But, it's ok now. Because we have learned they did it to keep us safe.

Mommy said she remembers how excited Sky was when he first pulled himself up to stand by holding onto the couch. And three months later, I, did the same thing too!

From the standing position, we would flop to the floor. We fell down a lot. Mommy would help us up, give us a kiss, and say, "it's ok". Then we would do it all over again.

While standing, we started to shuffle from side to side while holding onto the furniture. That is how we learned to cruise!

As we became more confident cruisers, we would cruise around the entire house. We held onto any and everything for support. But mainly, we held onto the walls, chairs, and tables.

Mommy said after Sky learned to cruise, he would yell and cry whenever she or daddy tried to hold his hands. Sky wanted to cruise by himself.

I did the opposite after I learned to cruise. Mommy and daddy would hold my hands to help me balance. I would only cry when they let go of my hands.

Mommy said, "one day Sky just took his first step without holding onto anything. He learned to waddle walk! Daddy was so happy, he shouted, "Yay", while clapping with excitement."

Five months later, I took my first step on my own. Daddy also shouted "Yay" and clapped with excitement.

When we both started to walk on our own, we would walk with our legs far apart and feet pointing outwards. Mommy said we walked like ducks to keep from falling down.

As we continued to move around the house, mommy and daddy also continued to childproof our house. They moved all the tall, wobbly, and sharp furniture out of our reach. They put baby gates on the stairs to keep us safe.

They put stove and cabinet knob covers everywhere, except for one cabinet. I think they purposely left that one. It's the one with the plastic bowls and our secret playing place.

Mommy said Sky and I learned to walk at our own time and at our own pace. She said after a few months of waddle walking, our muscles, balance, and confidence improved. We started to walk like big kids!

Mommy said walking is a long process that we learned over time. We walked when we were ready. Before we were able to walk, we had to build strong muscles, learn how to sit up, roll over, scoot, crawl, cruise, waddle, and then we walked!

Now we can also run, jump, climb and play all day.

SEE YOU NEXT TIME WHEN WE LEARN THE ABC's!

www.ingramcontent.com/pod-product-compliance
Lightning Source LLC
Chambersburg PA
CBHW060900270326

41935CB00003B/47

9 781957 319018